GREAT CAREERS IN ENGINEERING

by Meg Gaertner

FOCUS READERS

NAVIGATOR

WWW.FOCUSREADERS.COM

Focus Readers is distributed by North Star Editions:
sales@northstareditions.com | 888-417-0195

Produced for Focus Readers by Red Line Editorial.

Photographs ©: Shutterstock Images, cover, 1, 4–5, 8–9, 11, 13, 14–15, 17, 18, 22–23, 25, 26–27; Xi Jianxin/Imagine China/AP Images, 21; Red Line Editorial, 29

Library of Congress Cataloging-in-Publication Data
Names: Gaertner, Meg, author.
Title: Great careers in engineering / by Meg Gaertner.
Description: Lake Elmo, MN : Focus Readers, [2022] | Series: Great careers | Includes index. | Audience: Grades 4-6
Identifiers: LCCN 2021001377 (print) | LCCN 2021001378 (ebook) | ISBN 9781644938430 (hardcover) | ISBN 9781644938898 (paperback) | ISBN 9781644939352 (ebook) | ISBN 9781644939772 (pdf)
Subjects: LCSH: Engineering--Vocational guidance--Juvenile literature.
Classification: LCC TA157 .G3234 2022 (print) | LCC TA157 (ebook) | DDC 620.0023--dc23
LC record available at https://lccn.loc.gov/2021001377
LC ebook record available at https://lccn.loc.gov/2021001378

Printed in the United States of America
Mankato, MN
082021

ABOUT THE AUTHOR

Meg Gaertner is a children's book writer and editor. She loves learning about advances made in science, medicine, and engineering. When not writing, editing, or learning, she can be found swing dancing or hiking the forests of Minnesota.

TABLE OF CONTENTS

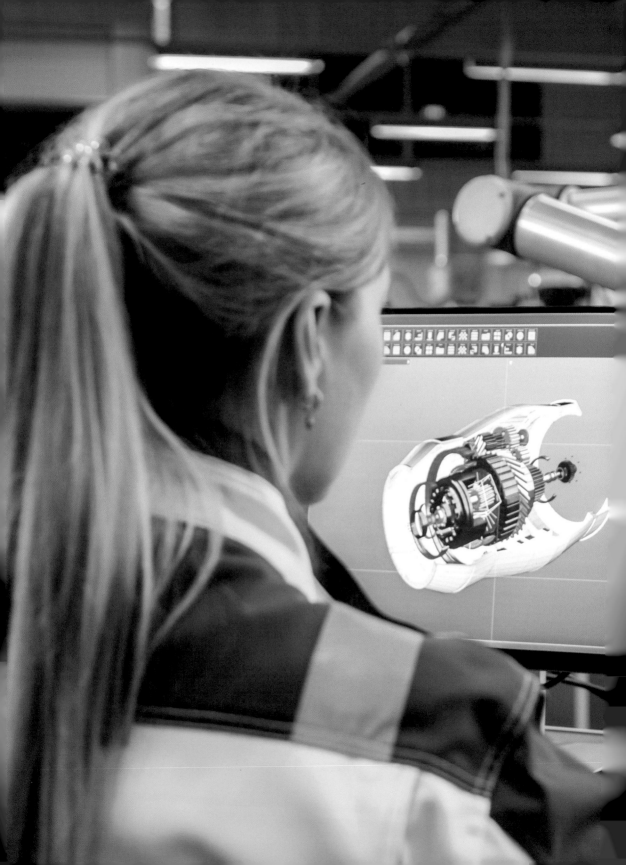

CHAPTER 1

WHAT DO ENGINEERS DO?

Engineers use math and science to solve problems. Often, this process involves **designing** machines or structures. Machines include cars and computers. Structures include buildings and bridges. Engineers even design whole systems. In a system, many parts connect to form a whole. The parts also affect one

A mechanical engineer uses a computer to design an engine.

another. For example, a city's roads form a system. Traffic on one road can affect movement on nearby roads. Engineers plan systems to work smoothly.

There are many different kinds of engineers. Some design bridges and buildings. Others design tools for the

LEARNING THE BASICS

Engineers study the **physical** world and how it works. They study sciences such as physics and chemistry. Physics is the science of matter, movement, and energy. It looks at the basic building blocks of matter. It studies how objects move. And it studies how energy changes forms. Chemistry also studies matter. It looks at how matter changes. In addition, it looks at creating new substances.

human body. Some engineers work to improve cars. Others design robots to do different tasks. But all engineers work to solve problems and benefit humankind.

BRANCHES OF ENGINEERING

MECHANICAL

- Aerospace Engineering
- Biomedical Engineering
- Automotive Engineering

CIVIL

- Structural Engineering
- Architectural Engineering
- Transportation Engineering

ELECTRICAL

- Computer Engineering
- Electronics Engineering
- Robotics Engineering

CHEMICAL

- Environmental Engineering
- Materials Engineering
- Agricultural Engineering

MANAGEMENT

- Industrial Engineering
- Systems Engineering
- Manufacturing Engineering

GEOTECHNICAL

- Petroleum Engineering
- Geological Engineering
- Mining Engineering

CHAPTER 2

CIVIL AND MECHANICAL

Civil engineers design and build **infrastructure**. Some civil engineers design buildings or bridges. Some plan roads, railroads, subway systems, or airports.

Other civil engineers build cities' water-supply systems. Pipes carry clean water to people's sinks and showers.

Building a bridge requires huge amounts of planning.

Engineers build waste-removal systems, too. Pipes carry dirty water away. Civil engineers also design power stations. They build the infrastructure to deliver electricity to homes and businesses.

SURVEYORS AND CARTOGRAPHERS

Civil engineers need large amounts of information for their designs. They get that information from others. For example, surveyors measure the land. They also determine who owns a plot of land. Cartographers make and update maps. Some of these are maps of Earth's surface. Others are maps of where people live. These maps show how many people live in certain areas. All of this information helps civil engineers decide where and how to build.

Civil engineers work with architects and construction companies to make sure structures are built properly.

Whatever their focus, civil engineers first create many designs. The designs show where and how something should be built. Engineers want infrastructure to last a long time. They want it to be safe. And they want infrastructure that won't damage the environment. Civil engineers choose the best plan. Then they work with others to carry it out.

Mechanical engineers design products and machines. They work on products that involve mechanical processes. A huge variety of products fall into this category. Some engineers design spaceships, airplanes, or military ships. Others work in the medical field. They design medical tools. Some of these tools help doctors detect health problems. Others are devices that can save lives.

Some mechanical engineers work in manufacturing and **automation**. They design machines that build products. They develop control systems. These

Some mechanical engineers help design the robots that build cars.

computers allow machines to operate without human help.

Mechanical engineers work to lower the cost of making things. They also try to make the building process more **efficient**. Engineers want products to be safe and long-lasting. And they want products that are not harmful to the environment.

CHAPTER 3

CHEMICAL AND ELECTRICAL

Chemical engineers focus on chemical processes. In these processes, matter changes form. Chemical engineers often take raw matter and make it more useful.

Chemical engineers work in many different fields. Some make foods healthier and tastier. Or they make foods last longer. Others develop ways

A chemical engineer performs many tests to find out which methods work best.

to produce drugs for treating illnesses. Some engineers make better fuels. Others focus on clean water and air. They work to control pollution. And they develop better ways to recycle.

Many chemical engineers design new **materials**. They often try to create materials that are lighter and stronger. They also create materials that are better for the environment. People use these materials to make new products.

Chemical engineers also design materials for the medical field. Some people need medical devices inside their bodies. However, the human body will reject many materials. For this reason,

Chemical engineers help design artificial heart valves that go inside people's bodies.

chemical engineers must make materials that the body will not reject.

Electrical engineers design, build, and maintain electrical systems. These systems include power, communication, and navigation systems. Power systems involve equipment that creates power, such as motors. Wires bring that power to

Without electrical engineers, devices such as phones and tablets would not exist.

homes and businesses. Communication systems allow people to make phone calls and send text messages. They also allow people to send information over the internet. Navigation systems help people get to where they're going.

Electrical engineers also design electronic devices. These devices include computers and cell phones. They include TVs and video game consoles, too. Cars, airplanes, and ships have electrical parts as well. Electrical engineers design them.

ENGINEERING TECHNICIANS

Engineers do not work alone. Engineering technicians support them. These jobs exist in every engineering field. For example, technicians carry out the plans made by civil engineers. They help mechanical and electrical engineers by testing products. They make sure the products work. And they repair the products if there are problems. In general, engineering technician jobs require less education. And they are quicker to enter into.

BIONICS

A bionic limb is a type of artificial body part. For instance, a person without a lower arm can wear a bionic arm. Bionic arms are shaped like natural arms. They run on batteries. The fingers can grip and hold things. They enable users to do many everyday activities. For example, people with bionic arms can pick up food and brush their teeth.

Several kinds of engineers work together to build a bionic arm. Mechanical engineers play a role. The arm involves separate pieces that connect. These pieces form the fingers and hand. Motors in the arm make the pieces move.

Electrical engineers also contribute. A user's muscles give off electrical signals. The arm picks up those signals. It turns them into movement. The fingers on the hand open or close.

Making a bionic arm involves several different types of engineering.

The arm involves software as well. The software tells tiny computers in the arm how to operate. By working together, engineers help people who need artificial limbs.

CHAPTER 4

GEOTECHNICAL AND MANAGEMENT

Geotechnical engineers study the movement of soil and rocks. They make sure infrastructure is safe from landslides and rockfalls. They also make sure people build on stable ground.

Other engineers focus on the ground, too. Earth has many natural resources. They include metals for manufacturing.

Geotechnical engineers study the ground to make sure it is safe to build on.

They also include oil and natural gas for producing power. Engineers help people remove these resources safely. Some engineers design mines. Others focus on safe ways to drill for oil or natural gas.

Manufacturing requires workers and machines. It also requires materials and energy. Management engineers oversee this whole process. They make the process more efficient and less costly. To do so, they might design a new work space. Or they might change how workers use their time.

Other engineers protect workers. They work to prevent injuries and accidents. They make sure workplaces are safe.

Manufacturing engineers help make sure factories run as efficiently as possible.

They also test the safety of machines and tools. Some engineers protect the people who buy products. To do so, they test the products before they are sold in stores. They make sure products are safe for people to use.

CHAPTER 5

ENTERING THE FIELD

There are many types of engineers. For each type, getting a job involves a similar process. Engineering technician jobs require an associate's degree. This degree usually takes two years to get. Engineering jobs require a four-year bachelor's degree. Many schools offer engineering degrees.

Young engineers often work with experienced engineers to learn the job.

People take entry-level jobs after finishing school. In these jobs, they work under experienced engineers. That way, young engineers can learn on the job. They gain experience.

Many engineers get licensed. This means they take tests through the government. With a license, they become professional engineers (PEs). PEs can take on leadership roles.

Some engineers go to graduate school. With a graduate degree, they can teach at universities. They can also do **research**.

Whatever the job, certain skills are important for engineers. For example, engineers are good at science and math.

They think critically. They solve problems. And they are often creative. Engineers work with **complex** information. They make it understandable. The engineering field has many opportunities. Being an engineer is a rewarding career.

CAREER PREP CHECKLIST

Interested in a career in engineering? As you move into middle school and high school, try these steps.

1 Take classes in science, especially chemistry and physics.

2 Take classes in math, including algebra, trigonometry, and calculus.

3 Read books on engineers and their jobs. Ask a librarian for help finding these books.

4 Tell your school's guidance counselor about your interest. This person can help you find opportunities to get experience in engineering.

5 See if your area has summer camps or after-school programs in science and engineering. Use the internet to find these opportunities.

FOCUS ON
GREAT CAREERS
IN ENGINEERING

Write your answers on a separate piece of paper.

1. Write a paragraph explaining the main ideas of Chapter 5.

2. What type of engineering do you think is most interesting? Why?

3. Which engineers focus on designing a city's physical infrastructure?

    A. mechanical
    B. civil
    C. electrical

4. Which engineers might work together to make a robot that can perform tasks?

    A. civil and chemical engineers
    B. mechanical and geotechnical engineers
    C. electrical and mechanical engineers

Answer key on page 32.

GLOSSARY

automation
The use of machines that can work without human control.

complex
Difficult to understand, and often involving many parts.

designing
Making a detailed plan for something before building it.

efficient
Accomplishing as much as possible with as little effort or as few resources as possible.

infrastructure
The structures, such as roads and bridges, that a city needs to function.

materials
The matter, such as cloth or metal, from which a thing can be made.

mechanical
Related to tools or machines.

physical
Related to things that are made of matter.

research
The act of studying something to learn more about it.

TO LEARN MORE

BOOKS

Eboch, M. M. *Mechanical Engineering in the Real World.*
   Minneapolis: Abdo Publishing, 2017.
Enz, Tammy. *Structural Engineering: Learn It, Try It!*
   North Mankato, MN: Capstone Press, 2018.
Farndon, John. *Stickmen's Guide to Engineering.*
   Minneapolis: Lerner Publications, 2018.

NOTE TO EDUCATORS

Visit **www.focusreaders.com** to find lesson plans, activities, links, and other resources related to this title.

INDEX

Answer Key: **1.** Answers will vary; **2.** Answers will vary; **3.** B; **4.** C

GREAT CAREERS

It's hard to know what to be when you grow up, especially because many options aren't obvious. This practical series highlights some of the jobs available in popular fields, describing what each job typically involves and the training required to pursue it.

BOOKS IN THIS SET

GREAT CAREERS IN EDUCATION

GREAT CAREERS IN ENGINEERING

GREAT CAREERS IN HEALTH CARE

GREAT CAREERS IN MUSIC

GREAT CAREERS IN NATURE

GREAT CAREERS IN SCIENCE

GREAT CAREERS IN SPORTS

GREAT CAREERS IN TECHNOLOGY

GREAT CAREERS IN WRITING

GREAT CAREERS WORKING WITH ANIMALS

Focus Readers deliver captivating topics, accessible text, and vibrant visuals to build reading confidence and motivate young readers.

NAVIGATOR
RL: 3–5. IL: 4–7.

NOTE TO EDUCATORS
Visit www.focusreaders.com to find:
- Lesson plans
- Activities
- Links
- Other resources related to this title

ISBN: 978-1-64493-889-8
90000

9 781644 938898